A PLAUSIBLE LIGHT

PAUL SMYTH

A Plausible Light

New and Collected Poems

EL LEÓN LITERARY ARTS

Berkeley · California 🙿

❧ Poems in this selection first appeared in The Atlantic Monthly, The Christian Science Monitor, Cyphers (Dublin), The Kenyon Review, The Lyric, Mississippi Review, The Sewanee Review, and the following in Poetry: "Ave, Vale"; "Of Scholarship, Divorce, and Lunch"; "Day Moon"; "After the Windstorm"; "An Elm Leaf"; "Desert Watch"; "A Box Turtle"; "A Gift"; the twelve-poem sequence, "Of His Affliction"; the eight-poem sequence, "Abraham at the Ruins of Hai." A number of the poems first appeared in Conversions, University of Georgia Press, 1974.

❧ El León Literary Arts is a nonprofit public benefit corporation established to extend the array of voices essential to a democracy's arts and education. The Overbrook Foundation's generous support is gratefully acknowledged.

❧ El León Literary Arts is distributed by Small Press Distribution, Inc., 800-869-7553; www.spdbooks.org.

❧ El León books are also available on Amazon.com

❧ El León web site: www.elleonliteraryarts.org

❧ Publisher: Thomas Farber; Managing Editor: Kit Duane; Editor: Helen Lang; Book Designer and frontispiece art: Barry Moser

❧ ISBN 978-0-9762983-1-1

❧ Library of Congress Number 2007924100

CONTENTS

III. Domicles

IV. At Large

V. TENTATIVE

CODA

A PLAUSIBLE LIGHT

A BLADE OF DUNE GRASS

A blade of dune grass bends to etch the sand
A life-long foot from where its roots take hold;
The source is circumscribed, a motion told,
The blade has marked the space of its windy stand.

It's wind that moves the supple grass to write
But the selfsame wind erases all that's said—
The circling blade must struggle to keep ahead,
To keep the word intact around its site.

Through all the winds and weathers of the year
Its life and dying share a single move
As graceful as an unthought move in love.
And now we pause to kneel and witness here
The word of being spoken pure, a voice
Uncluttered by a judgement or a choice.

I. PRIMER

SOME THOUGHTS OF THAT

still stand upright,
the way ancient pillars might stand
through countless turns of wind and sun
on a high green plateau,

tall columns smoothed,
bleached beyond white
to bone pureness of age,

surprising to an old shepherd
after the steep trails up
from winter pastures,
known, yet
sudden in his bright morning

causing him
to let his sheep graze,
for a moment to lean on his stick
pondering silent things that persist

upright, yet
barely able even to indicate
a whole story as they shine
unattended in the clear air.

THE GREENFIELD

We named it out of young immediate sense
For chest-high grass that swept the eyes and nose,
Not for the weathered granite rock that rose
Central, silent, proud, creviced, immense.

We stormed the rock for a pirates' brigantine.
Daily we sailed uncharted summer seas
Bound for the islands past the hemlock trees,
Bound for the farthest latitudes of green,

Till the day the two red haying tractors came.
We sat still on the rock watching their slow
And ever-closer circling laying low
Our deep green field. We whispered the fallen name,

And at dusk we limped a barefoot stubble-walk
Home from the field, home from the looming rock.

A GIRL AT DAWN

She moves upon
these public garden paths
like a sigh moving through darkness,
pressing and giving way,

and in the easy motion of her passing
she seems, herself,
a phase of the coming dawn,
more natural event than girl,
more than in pure coincidence with light.

She moves as a sigh would
along the edges of lawns,
near benches, circles once
around the still pavilion,

then, by careful steps,
to the bank of the dark duck pond
where she stops, leaning
as if she would commit
some word upon the water—

from the far center of the pond
ripples spread like echo toward her,
she turns, the garden wakes
pale green and cool in mists
that half-dissolve her effortless retreat.

THE HOUSE

Far on the outer beach the strange hulk stands,
A belly-laugh at architectural grace—
It reaches, juts and sprawls, grabs chunks of space,
It rises like a chorus of demands.

It's pieced of driftwood, every beam and board;
The second floor looms larger than the first;
Its upward thrust seems doomed to be reversed
By all the laws of physics and discord.

Yet up it stays, like a fool's philosophy.
Created of scraps the storm-tide put at hand
It now shouts rude defiance to the sea
While struggling to keep its feet on shifting sand.
That there's some power that keeps it none can doubt,
Some logic moving like love—from inside out.

TWO ON A DELTA MARSH

In the beginning there were great separations,
and the evenings and the mornings were the days.

1.
Dawn on the great salt marsh comes doubly gray,
Thick by dew falling and steam rising.
Reluctantly the night begins to give,
Day finds a pale way among tall grasses
And damp salt smells,
Lighting, too, a gull's cry
And a river that ripples its last hours
Thin and hesitant near the sea.

These are slow hours.
Blossoms yield to fruit,
A thousand tiny scents swell.

Since by bright light the world's not seen,
And since night, too, is exclusive,
We start with the simplest—

This hour, this marsh
Where all is firm and damp
And light and dark at once.

We approach the third day first.

2.

These are slow hours
But hours nonetheless,
Mocking stopped clocks with minds
Open to know, anxious to remember.

Before the sun comes,
Before one blade of grass is wholly known,
Before the first petal falls,
What part of all the life
Emerging from this dawn will slip away?

Soon we will be at home
Crowding the woodstove,
Removing wet clothes,
Toweling steam and dew from our hair
And breakfasting quietly,

But first, this hour.
We swirl the mists around us as we move,
The air of every breath is gray.
Our wet steps carry us beyond our voices—
There is no word to speak,
Nothing to laugh, nothing to cry.

If mind could be the mist among such grass...

We approach the third day first,
The day of separation making way for life.

3.
We try to feel the genesis of life,
Hoping to encounter—in this dawn, this marsh—
The dim source of what we are, the source
Of the cherished self.

What can we know this morning?

Whatever can be known is here,
For we are here, you and I,
Gathering unto ourselves the sum of our experience.

We know that hours can be dense and slow.

We move toward home
Through air turning brilliant white

As a great blue heron unfurls his bulk,
Gathers his strength and lifts his awkward body,
Strains into the air,
Following the river-course beyond the continent,

Marking,
By steady undulation of his wings,
The slow rhythm of silent passage.

A FEAR

Like two who for support share measured lies
Trusting to some arrival far ahead,
These railroad tracks endure their cinder bed
Spiked firmly down on creosoted ties.

The rusting rails stretch level toward the bend
Securely held together yet apart—
They speak that life of parallels my heart
Has anguished in but could not comprehend.

Now twice a week the night freight rumbles by
Screeching and clacking like some significant weight,
But always empty, always an hour late.
Then the singing in the rails fades to a sigh
As the freight moves on toward the locked last station where
A yellow light bulb sickens the platform air.

OUR LADY

"Why, then, do you pray to me? You summon life
But speak of loving only, darkness of soil
And white roots winding among stones, of earth
Where you have drawn your passion's nourishment.
Love must embrace more than the struggle of loving.
Speak of the exile,

"Speak of the hour of silence. This morning, alone:
Was it autumn, and you in a withered garden, you
Cutting the dry stalks? Or, naked at the mirror,
Aware first of your hands, then of breasts and hips,
Did conception melt you? Did the violet light of genesis
Flash through your body?"

"Madonna, I felt only the familiar light,
The steady bulb, cool, as in a florist's
Refrigerated showcase. My body was full
With roses, with the hush of a million crisp petals,
And I heard, somewhere, an electric motor humming,
Keeping the fragrance."

PORTRAIT

He prowls the city at night
Or sometimes the beach at night
Looking up alleys
Or behind breakwaters
Searching, always searching for his eyes.

Those two acetylene torch nozzles
In his head cut great, gaping holes
In fog, women, doors,
As though his eyes might. . .might
This time be in there, waiting

To be found, picked up, replaced
In his head (he would junk
The torches), but this time placed in
Correctly, facing out at the world
Not backwards looking into scars and blood

The way they were at birth,
That way he endured them for years,
That way he finally couldn't any longer
And tore them out, mushy, pale from what they'd seen.
But now, where did they go

When he growled and heaved them
Tears and all, stringy, into blackness?
He prowls now, still wiping his hands
On his pants, searching, burning gaping holes,
Forgetting a lot, missing a lot,

On the beach more now,
Timing the tides now
As though he considers moving in,
Living there, alone, in the dark,
Searching, always searching for his eyes.

A CRUCIAL BRAILLE

My fingers tremble near what I would touch
But hesitate, then fail, like children nearing
The coffin of someone finally loved too much,
Like old men when they hear the children sneering.

These fingers once redeemed a fluttering bird
Too tightly, in a fist: for years I have known
That heart-like pulse subsiding, and known the word
For holding to death a thing that might have flown.

The crucial Braille of frost on this windowpane
Shrinks from my touch. Is it enough to hold
My fingers only *near* the glass, to gain
No entrance to the testament of cold?
Yet my own life reserves itself that much.
My fingers tremble near what I would touch.

ROAD CONSTRUCTION

Each morning I'd start the compressor, a yellow HERMES,
And pack the shank in grease. The hammer weighed
Ninety-five pounds, and the drivers stood in threes
Nodding and spitting, lean, relaxed, well paid.
The thick-faced foreman muttered studying
His rolled-out blueprints' eight abstracted lanes.
His brute D-9's ate hills, and they could wring
fierce arias from rock by treads and chains.

My job was drilling holes for dynamite,
Staying slightly ahead of the highway's thrust.
I traded days for pay. I dreaded night.
Hunched in the din, in the clouds of granite dust,
My jackhammer beating deeply into the ledge,
I labored at the future's crumbling edge.

IN CLOUDS OF GLARE

The eye discerns
One spectrum's range, but comes to know
Another need it serves:
The eye adapts toward vision, learns
What light may undergo
Deep in the brain. The light that swerves
Through optic nerves

Flutters alive
On crane-booms, trucks, on girders blue
As night, and vision scales
Scaffolds where, somehow, workmen survive
Light's ecstasy on new
Coiled cable, planks, red balcony rails
And polyethylene sails.

A hubcap swells
Captive pedestrians, retards
Desire: the eye is drawn
Into its whorl where shoppers dwell
As liquids, where vision guards
Illogic till—a whole world gone—
The car moves on.

This sunlight squeaks
On chrome, this city glints and shines,
Wide spectra caught and bent
In steel and glass, and silver shrieks

Of light pierce buttons, stop signs,
Hydrants, spires—all things consent
To ravishment

By light: each sings
The other, surfaces celebrate
Reflected edges, turns
Of form—embracing form, light wrings
The breath from bulk and weight
In clouds of glare: the moist eye learns
Its need, and burns.

THE ESCAPED

live off the land.
They get fresh meat by guile
and sticks and stones, they understand
by adverbs, *how* and *while*.
They're out there: vile,

starving, obsessed
with darkness, swamp, and ledge,
freedom their only fire and rest.
They mock the sheriff's pledge,
red teeth on edge.

FACE TO FACE

1.

Last year, at Christmas, I asked my brother why
He'd run away when he was fourteen, gone
Six bewildering months before they sent him

Home from Florida in handcuffs. "Are you *kidding?*"
He spit it, his face twisting ugly and flushed.
He meant our stepfather, he meant living in fear

Of daily pain, the terrible, terrible beatings.
He began to say more, but didn't, his mouth
Went white and tightened, his eyes glazed and burned

With furious hatred, hatred decades old.
I changed the subject, embarrassed by his pain,
But thought all afternoon about the miraculous

Power of metaphor to save our lives.
He has none, none at all, only a white
Mercedes, expensive tailored suits, money

To bet heavily and, if he wishes, to burn.

2.

When I was a boy we had no furnace, only
five fireplaces and endless need for wood.
All summer my brother and I felled trees and cut

The thirteen cords or more we'd burn each winter.
My left foot high, bracing the log in the sawbuck,
I'd work, the bucksaw blade slicing the grain,

My right foot deep in sawdust, morning dew
Sweet on the wood-smell. Ax, sledgehammer, wedges,
We worked into November, and it got cold.

Christ, we were young. Our father's despair had been
Made death, our stepfather huge, violent, drunk,
And when we bent to the two-man crosscut saw

It blurred with motion, moaned and sang, the blade
Our steel-toothed daily fear, the trunks of oaks
Hard, knotted, and heavy as a father lost.

Christ, we were proud of every cord we stacked.

3.
One February night the temperature sank
To −20°, and the water pump froze.
I clambered down to the cellar to get it going,

Down through the trap door in the kitchen floor,
Down rickety steps to cobwebs, stones,
The dirt floor, the frozen musty odors.

I cleaned the kerosene space heater, changed the wick,
And lugged the two-gallon tank upstairs. Outside,
My eyes stung in the cold. And, there in the dark,

The dry snow squeaking beneath my boots, hunched
Behind the woodshed, bent to the oil drum's spigot,
I watched the spumes of Northern Lights above me:

There in the black sky washes of green,
Silver, red, like imagination itself
Rising over the frozen world. I shivered,

Swayed in the spectral thought: *my life, my life.*

4.
I walk over the dunes where telegraph poles
Are skinny crosses, a long wavering column
Held up, it seems, by the wires strung between them,

The poles and crossbars black against the still
Drifting of sand, the wires invisible
Until I walk near them, beneath them, wondering

About the coded messages tapped out
By Coast Guard personnel—a danger of shipwreck,
An enemy submarine, or, I wonder,

Some mention of a man whose ashes once
Were scattered here, blowing over the sand.
I stand beneath the wires listening, the wind

A moaning in them, a moaning along the wires
Or someone crying, crying, crying a need
That wind and sand have not begun to answer,

The long moaning from cross to cross to cross.

5.
The spring that I was five I found in the woods
Far in back of our house a little dump.
A pile of rusty cans, bottles, and one

Treasure: an Underwood typewriter, ancient, rusty,
Rusted solid in fact. But the black keys
Had not rusted, the Bakelite or whatever it was

Had held the letters legible there in the woods,
And I, who knew the alphabet, had stared
Dumbfounded at that mysterious order. *No wonder,*

No wonder they threw it out, the letters are all
Mixed up. I hunted for A and B and C
And through to z touching them one by one.

I remained dumbfounded long after I'd asked
And learned the reason for that disorder. The logic
I lacked there in the woods was, all along,

Right in the very structure of my hands.

6.

My ninth-grade science text revealed the world
Of radio waves, long waves and short and how
Transmitters and receivers work. Our radio

At home was old, cabinet-style with fabric
Over the speaker, and smelled of heat and dust,
But it had a shortwave band. I strung a wire

Across the lawn from tree to house, fixing
The glass insulators, screwing the lead wire to
The radio's back and, finally, turning it on:

The sky was alive with language, the atmosphere
Awash with eerie pulses, and late at night
I crouched over it, my cheek pressed to the wood,

The scent of warm varnish and the orange glow
Of a dozen tubes tinting the bodiless voices
Rushing across the stars—French from Quebec,

Spanish from Quito, and always the intricate static.

7.

The sign above me said, *Moore's Monuments Inc.,*
And I knelt in its shadow, ten years old,
Laboring at a polished granite surface

With bucket and brush and chemical solution.
I scrubbed weather stains from nameless gravestones
For fifty cents an hour for old Tom Moore.

My father had no marker, his ashes blowing
Over sand dunes. A hundred miles from there
I stared at the gray-black stone and saw my face

Beneath its surface, as vague and distant as
The memory of certain sounds, of surf,
My image moving where someone's father's name

Would be sandblasted beneath the fine vignette
Of leafy vines that represented life.
I scrubbed it harder, and as I worked I watched
My face rise to the surface, face to face.

II. THEN AND NOW

MY FATHER'S LEDGER

Here is the red account in his cramped hand,
　　　Straight columns side by side,
The losses figured nightly. Life and land
　　　That year before he died
Shriveled to less than half what he had planned,

To a tenth of what he hoped, a hundredth part
　　　Of what the earliest pages
Conceive in joy. The heavy debits start,
　　　Replacements, paid-out wages,
The graph-curves each pursue a sinking heart.

Post forty-nine percent that reach dead ends,
　　　Then the forty-nine youth spent.
Beneath a fiery sword his ink defends
　　　That final two percent
Where struggle earns its steady dividends
　　　Of salt and punishment.
The figures grow illegible, then it ends.

SLIPPING INTO ST. STEPHEN'S CHAPEL

An Anniversary Votive

This sweet red trembling light
Above which shadows sprawl and lurch
May answer loss despite
My ignorance of Christ and Church

As, twenty-four years dead,
My father's name comes up once more.
My son, who's two, has said
Nothing of this. He'll soon be four.

How dark and cool God is,
How hushed, abstracted now: midweek,
Midday, the house all His
Except for solitudes that speak

In candles paid for, lit,
And trusted to keep a precious name.
At twenty-eight I sit
Close to the reasons why I came.

ELEGY

Paul Carleton Smyth, 1908-1948

He asked for fire
Believing love would burn
And grief expire;
And asked, for dying, his return
To sea and dunes. That heritage
Grows harder every year,
Three fading pages.

And also said:
"All things revive my grief
And mourn my dead;
The quivering of a shadowed leaf
Repeats my spirit's dying phrases."
I hear the leaves, and read
The shadowed pages.

The grief was named:
"The wave charges the beach
And, greatly tamed,
Recites in shrinking foam the speech
Of love's withdrawal." Love's homages
And shadowed leaves remain,
The fading pages,

And nothing more.
His death, perfected then,
Had come before—
I seek his voice but find again
Death's voice in living images.
All shadowed leaves restore
These fading pages.

VIGIL

The parking lot is empty except for me.
It's cold in the car, I'm smoking, staring out
Into the dusk, over the slate-blue sea.
It's overcast and windy. Father, I doubt
That you observed my bleak walking, and yet
I touched the frothy surf, the skiff of snow
Blowing over the sand, the violet
And umber seaweed, the white wing bone.
No,
I came because I need your voice again.
Three gulls are circling, two hunch on a rock.
The Atlantic looks miserable, it moans *Amen*
Over and over. The luminous dashboard clock
Says ten past five, the gulls now tilt and tack
Toward shore against the wind. I'll be back.

OF HIS AFFLICTION

Behold, I have refined thee, but not with silver;
I have chosen thee in the furnace of affliction.

ISAIAH 48:10

1.

You stand alone,
A broken wall, pine trees
Drive roots beneath the bleaching stone.
The steady hissing of disease
Seeps from the ground. And these,
The fruits of moments Fear has sown,
Fear on his hands and knees
With chips of bone.

2.

You crouched in a cave of grapevines, knelt toward the hum,
The field of insects, watching the thick dusk spread
Like anguish over a face—you who had come
Running through swollen woods, who lied then fled
To this field's edge, this frantic hum the same
As thin internal humming that scorched not ears
But lungs and brain, that sizzling you would name
The Locusts. You knelt at the edge of seven years,

Then stood, and pushing aside the veil of vines
Stepped into the field: instantly all sound ceased—
Except, as it rose from the dead tree slowly on
Enormous wings over the murky pines,
The crow cawed twice. For a moment, all memory gone,
You wore the silks of silence like a priest.

3.
       Always the threat,
    Downstairs, of violence—
Whiskey and frothy shouting; yet
Silence was worse, the creaking silence.
    And what was your offense?
Weakness: the kind that must beget
    An iron obedience
        Upon its debt.

       Lying in bed
    You heard his shouting rise
Around your name, a sound that led
To ruin, to facts like myths: his size,
    His strength, his fists, his eyes.
You listened to the brook instead,
    Its muddy compromise
        Of hope and dread.

How to prepare?
You watched the ceiling, tried
To gauge his voice. Time was your lair,
And night, where hope and dread collide
Crushing the minutes. Outside
The brook kept gurgling, unaware
Of his terrific stride
Leveling the stair.

4.

Like a pinball, shot and played against the slant:
roll down slip past two flippers clattering fall
into the trough but no so want to can't
green flippers red electric bumpers all
buzzing to touch and jingling on the board
back-bending neon girls flash as they smile
now carom flee this bumper's cringing chord
upping the score clicked index of denial

steel pinball chrome-skinned shot electric effect
know nothing else not volts not any cause
so flipped and spinning monad o reflect
whirl neon girls hot face of him who plays
his nickel's worth of what?—conceal steel's flaws
slick pinball chrome blushing with vivid praise.

5.
        Now live with pain,
    The god who flaps his way
Through sinew, joint, and wrinkled vein.
As close as breathing you obey
    Pain's scraping beak by day,
By night his caw. Your bones disdain
    The little prayers you weigh
        Like suet or grain

        But can't recite;
    You think of a grinning skull,
Also a speechless thing, then bite
Your lip to make deep pain seem dull
    Till sleep begins to pull,
To lure you in, till sleep seems right
    And even masterful.
        But in the night

        Your nerves, that twist
    Like roots down through your back
Begin the ruttish whines that mist
Your eyes with turpentine and crack
    Your skin—veins drip shellac,
Hot bubbling muscle-fibers kissed
    To tar. Shrunk hard and black,
        Your brain's a fist.

6.

In the wavy bathroom mirror rippling lay
five badge-like bruises: four fingerprints, the thumb.
He'd grabbed and held your throat like a fistful of clay.
Sick with pain and the smell of spilled Bay Rum
You winced touching those marks that seemed afloat
Like islands on your skin—his madness' map,
A clumsily worked projection of remote
Volcanic realms that would spread and overlap—

The blotch would be too hideous in school.
But the bus, your daily ark, could not be missed:
You readied yourself for playground ridicule
And washed your swollen face and buttoned your coat.
Then, in a last reflex of the will to resist,
You smeared your mother's makeup on your throat.

7.

         You knew so well
      The fist that crushed your lip,
Had watched so closely as it fell
Or rushed in level from his hip,
      That when that hand would grip
A chair-back angrily you could tell
      By a whitening knuckletip
         Degrees of hell.

You braided strings
To divine your labor's wage:
The strands revealed that famine brings
A time of plenty, that every rage
Must, more or less, presage
Delight. You counted your breaths, logs' rings,
Making each thing the gauge
Of other things,

And thought you could
Store years themselves away
With little loss: you cut the firewood,
Each cord a year, the loss a day
In sawdust. But the ash was gray,
Buckets of ashes; and you understood
That life is the price you pay
For livelihood.

8.
Trudging across the field you could not say
The sum of corn, exhaustion, peas, and heat.
You lowered the buckets for the hundredth time that day
Into the shallow brook: *Here two worlds meet.*
Over the stones and ooze of bottom slime
Flows water fat with life, with leafy plants
Whose white roots hold against the drag of time,
Resigned, resolved in undulating trance.

You looked deep in—past shiny browns and greens,
Past water and light and shadowy moving gloom,
Past metaphor: to one who kneels, who leans
Into the deepening breath, whose breathing slows—
Then turned, lifting the buckets, to resume
Soaking the twelfth of twenty dusty rows.

9.
            Why did you wait,
        Shy, in the clearing? There
No question asked could compensate
For those unasked in shrill fear
        Of sudden answers where
The world was rage. *It's getting late,*
    You and the cooler air
        Deliberate,

        But still no word.
    No voice responds here, none,
The woods keep silent. Now a bird
Questions the disappearing sun
    Bright edgy notes that run
Through heavy boughs. At dusk you heard
    The air's long sigh begun,
        A minor third

Raising the scent
Of withered grass and moss:
A dim hour paused, and bent
Slowly to gather up your loss,
The shadows cast across
Your lips with every breath, then went
Into the pines that toss
Bewilderment.

10.
You stand alone. A broken wall, pine trees
Drive roots into the sodden earth and drink.
Their boughs are dark with voices murmuring, "Please"—
Mere statement, not a request. Your seasons shrink
And hissing fade like a long wave's foam and froth.
Four billion years ago parched cells first sipped
Nutrition from the steaming primordial broth
Defining life, and entering the crypt

Of age and place forever. Now, you wait.
The past backs off, the future turns and flees.
You arrange the shriveled griefs, weigh what's left,
As a child will push cold peas around his plate.
Did those first cells drink to Charity or to Theft?
The pine boughs' ponderous tossing answers, "Please."

11.

Go back to the car,
Give up this hopeless thing,
Drive home. Wish on the blue-white star
For simple moonlight, fields that sing,
Declare that mornings bring
New reasons, clear as the minutes are.
Give up this hopeless thing.
It's gone too far.

Lying in bed
Imagine a chain-link fence
With barbed-wire gates, a tin-roofed shed,
Lean, iron-eyed guards who live in tents
Nearby. For all time hence
Let memories eat the meager bread
Of despair, each violence
Dying or dead.

How to prepare?
Fear rolls large flickering eyes,
Swings nimbly from rib to rib—"Beware!"
Kill him, feed him, muffle his cries—
A stack of heartbeats tries
Buying that hunchback out of there,
But fear is penny-wise
Screeching, "The stair!"

12.
You drive all night—a windshield wiper's arc,
The headlights' sprawl, and the ever-dying hiss
Of tires on wet asphalt. At dawn you park
And step from the car and stretch, embracing this:
Green picnic tables, trash cans, the silence of mist
Drifting among the trees, and beside the road
Two crows devouring flesh. Those years subsist
On your will to devise their final episode,

You cross wet grass toward where the dead thing lies.
The patient crows retreat to a nearby tree.
You kneel. It was a hound. His stomach is torn,
Neck twisted, mouth open howling silence. And his eyes,
Opaque and staring skyward: through them you see
That threat of which his abstract howls still warn.

THE BRUSH CUTTER

1.

He dreams immaculate fields and gardens—dreams
Abhorrent to nature as vacuums: scrub-brush and brambles
Would overtake his property, finally his house,
Ferns rooting under the bathtub, serpentine vines
Coiling up table legs and bedposts. He lies
Wide-eyed in bed just before sunrise, hearing
The cardinal through silver mists, the mourning dove,
The retiring owl, and the message of birdsong is
Explicit as a repossession notice,
As Kruschev pounding the U.N. table with his shoe.

2.

All day long he hacks at the brush, forcing
Nature's retreat back to meadow walls,
To lawn- and garden-borders, his steel tools
An arsenal von Clauswitz would understand
As metaphysics by other means, his work now
A skirmish with thorned encroachment, now quick arrest
Of thistles clustered beneath his windowsills.
He whistles a little as he works, a tactic
Exacting patience of cardinal and mourning dove,
Of owls deep in the woods who wink like scheming colonels.

3.

As creeping nature infiltrates his thought
Of what the spirit is and needs, ideas
Pale as the hearts of leeks, translucent words

Whose cultivation knobs and gnarls his fingers
Like ginger roots, pale words he seldom utters
For fear of their dissolving in the sweat
Of his own labor as evenings and mornings fail—
As green insinuations darken his knowledge
Of what the spirit is, he pauses, kneeling
Over narcissus beside the fungus-covered elm stump.

4.

He grips his growling chain saw as if it were
A yellow machine gun, and hours the belts of bullets,
He straddles ash trees where they've fallen crisscrossed
And strips their limbs off, cuts the trunks for firewood.
His finger squeezing the trigger, regulating
This engine to his purpose, he executes
His mission and his morning: slash and cordwood,
Deep drifts of white-gold sawdust at his feet,
He grips the throaty chain saw as if it were
His Book of Psalms, crouched in the mighty voice of David.

5.

This labor is sovereignty by other means,
His projects mapped, land policies defined
As if by Cabinets, his detailed agendas
For field and garden like aerial photographs
Prickling with multicolored pins, small flags,
Describing a state as free of brush as Plato's.
He might sit still at dusk, at peace, alone,
If nature be held subdued for just that instant

When light's in equipoise—no threat, no sentry,
Only the purpling twilight, scent of the damp ferns.

6.

Therefore he trenches the stream that every spring
Sprawls at the meadow's edge, the stream become
As undefined as thoughts about thinking—
He wants the water's flow confined, a *current*
Not water-sprawl that turns the lower meadow
Spongy, marshy as adolescent love.
He digs the trench; the overflow drains back.
Mattock and shovel, sweat, sweat in his eyes:
He watches the current sliding between his feet
As Magdalene once watched the troubled sleep of Jesus.

7.

He thinks of Yahweh and Moses where he labors,
Moses receiving the Law; but his stone tablets
Are chromosomes, looped laws that separate
And bind, and thought he bears toward darkness like
A quartz frieze of that hour he lies awake
Just before dawn, subpoenaed by the birdsong.
All day he testifies, hacking at brambles,
Piling them up, scratching his wrist and ankles.
He crowns the field with thorns which he will burn,
The fire snapping and crackling like Pilate's baffled conscience.

8.

The purple brambles lie in a tangled pile
Near where he walks among his apple trees,
The blue tank strapped to his back, the silver spray gun
A wand with which he touches every bough,
The misty silver spray like whisperings
Of souls gathered and waiting in his orchard.
He points the spray gun upward, circles the trees
As shadows deepen, his footsteps crunching on
The bramble stubble, his boots sticky with streaks
Of sap still bubbling up from the sheared-off purple stalks.

9.

At night he reads the news. The light bulb makes
A mirror of the window where he hears
Detailed stipulations tapped on the pane
By insects in love with light, a ticking code
Tapped on the image of his face, conditions
He knows he cannot meet. The vase at his elbow,
Empty all winter long, holds now a cloud
Of purple bloom: fragrance of lilacs fills
His mind with stipulations as the planet's
Dark side sighs, held in the heavy arms of green.

10.

He lies wide-eyed in bed just before sunrise.
Birdsong chisels his name on marbled mists.
As physics follows metaphysics, so
His waking into labor follows a dream—
This soldier of iris petal, axe-armed monk,

This partisan of boundaries, prayerful as
He twists goldenrod out of the earth for love
Of separations binding him to what
By circumstance he's come to call his spirit,
Holds in his mind the aerial views: maps, icons.

11.

Like a nihilistic orthodoxy sweeping
Nation on nation on in its whispering tide,
A moist green chaos greets this worker's hands
Who rises into daylight's dedications
With slow ablutions, with recitations of
Devotion that refracts in imagination—
He reaches for pencil and paper: things to be done.
That prismatic list in hand, he gazes out
That window where his reflection stymied insects
And which by daylight frames a garden, his name in bloom.

12.

Bound to his private stewardship, unsworn
Vocation woven of single blades of grass,
Of flower petals, of scent of the damp earth,
This surgeon of seasons shoulders axe and sledge,
Shoulders the spade and hoe. He who will heal
The land whose spirit is the dream he dreams
Advances, mute disciple of a labor
As intricate as time is. He marshals his being
Against the unruly shape of nature's advance,
Presses the weight of his body against it, leaf by leaf.

III. DOMICILES

TWO LOVERS IN THE LATE TRIASSIC
Museum of Natural History, New York

Remember that stunned pause in happiness?
Dwarfed by the skeletons of Tyrannosaurs
We felt God's grief. We groped for words to bless

With purpose life's remove to nothingness,
We played the taped accounts of trials and failures.
Remember that stunned pause in happiness

Near glassed-in swamps? A glance, and we could guess
How hungry they were, those red-eyed armored boars.
We felt God's grief, we groped for words to bless

Extinguished forms with reasoned cause and, yes,
With mercy. Again and again my hand found yours.
Remember that stunned pause in happiness

Near carnivores, who starved? Baffled, they witness
Flesh and blood stroll past and out the doors.
We felt God's grief, we groped for words to bless

Each other's lives. I felt your fingers press
And probe my palm for bones and metaphors.
Remember that stunned pause. In happiness
We felt God's grief. We groped for words to bless.

APOLOGY

Once, waging that dream, crying, crying
From drenched sleep the barbed cry of fear,
I frightened you.

Here is a split cocoon, still damp
With the damp of deep change, the labor of
A furry worm,

And near it the damp butterfly,
Wavering, walking a little on crooked legs,
Unused to wings.

A VALENTINE

I give you irises, by which I mean
To symbolize (and so not be obscene)
    Your innermost event.
    Quickly you have bent
To savor them, you blush as if you'd seen

The image of what blooms moonlit between
Your temples when the moon's a tambourine
    Shook by astonishment.
      I give you irises

And, like a courtier to his sighing queen,
I whisper, *At your service*, as you lean
    Toward me with no intent
    Save that blooming I meant
To symbolize. By which, I think, you mean
      I give you irises.

ELEMENTS OF LIGHT

1.

I think of this: I'm nine years old, sitting
Cross-legged beside a pond where minnows school—
A grassy bank, the sunstruck bottom-pebbles,
A half-sunken log. Here, in late afternoons
Fragrant with summer's sighing, green to green,
I sometimes grab for minnows, roiling the surface,
And watch the scattering silver fish regroup
A yard beyond my reach, and drifting back.
I never catch a minnow. I daydream where,
Toward dusk, the water darkens and fish are shadows.

2.

My son has found a muddy black rock
Studded with quartz crystals which, he hopes,
Are something really precious. Mine is to say
It's only quartz, and his to repeat the word
And wander off to find his hammer, reduced
From treasure-finder now, a boy who's got
Two dozen shiny crystals to chip and pocket.
He'll tap each crystal lightly, snapping it off,
Then scrub them in the bathroom sink. He'll tell
Himself and his friends that quartz is really jewels.

And I go back to digging out the stump
Which was our elm. Dutch elm disease destroyed it.
I sweat over pick and shovel, around and around it,
Down through the topsoil, down through hardpan clay,

Digging among wet roots that grip the earth
As desperately, as massively as the motives
That gripped the troubled heart of Abraham.
Soon, I'll cut the taproot beneath the stump,
But now my son leaps from the porch—running,
Crying, *Look!* His open palm adazzle.

3.

I think of this: an infrared film, a movie
Of some suburban house, heat leaking out
Around the door and windows, under the eaves,
A plume of heat wavering over the chimney
Blurring the silver television antenna,
The heat a smoldering, shimmering red that is
Slowly escaping, escaping even the silent
Image that fills the screen. I close my eyes
And imagine a man bursting out of the door,
Stumbling, his arms laden with burning books.

4.

A bottle of soapy water and a plastic blower
Are all my daughter needs to make the lawn
A swirl of gladness. She, no taller than
The columbine, releases streams of bubbles,
Small ones, large ones, a rising of reds and blues.
They float over the lilac bush, and she
Is all delight, chasing them, filling the air
With galaxies that rise on her warm breath.
Daddy! she cries, as a big one comes my way.
One by one they pop high in the trees.

Sometimes I watch her sleeping, faint breathing
Stirring the white fur of the stuffed toy cat
That she adores above all others. I watch
Her simple sleep, and I am afraid, and helpless.
But now, as I chop the roots, sweating, the air
Is brilliant, vivid with magic and happy noise,
As if all sleep were over, forever rescinded,
As if our fate would truly be undone
By this before my eyes. My palms are blistered,
Arms aching. The bubble-blower shakes in my hand.

5.

I think of this: a tribe crossing the desert
At night, fifty or sixty people, goats,
Mules laden with tents and bronze cooking pots.
The moon is full, the slow caravan winds
Along a silvered wadi. I hear the hooves
And feet scraping the stony ground, they move
Without talking, eastward, where soon a thin
White light will silhouette the bare horizon.
An infant whimpers, the mother answers something,
Then silence again, the steady hoof- and footfalls.

6.

I crouch beside the hibachi to turn the fish,
A thick filet of scrod, and butter sizzles,
Splattering onto the glowing charcoal. I flex
My hands and feel the broken blisters tingling.
With a two-by-four for a lever I heaved the stump

Out of the muddy hole and rolled it, wrestled it
Across the lawn to the drive. Now it lies there
Like some improbable deep-sea monster, beached.
My wife examines the dark wound in our lawn,
Pensive, her hand at her hair, then calls to the children,

Who, in bathing suits now, are giggling, running
Under the lawn sprinkler, back and forth, pleading
Just once more, once more, just once. I watch
Through the shimmering air above the charcoal fire,
Watch the way the sprinkler, leaning westward,
Bends in its arch of spray a miniature rainbow
Through which the children scamper one last time.
They go in to change. It's six o'clock, the lawn
Is golden in sunlight, pale violet in shadow.
Swallows dip and dart, stitching the air.

7.

There is no moon tonight, but starlight silvers
Roof and treetops. The yard is mottled with shadow,
The stump hole now a pool of dark in the dark.
The air is utterly still and clear. I walk
Barefoot across the damp grass, and pause,
Searching the sky: The Dippers, the Pleiades,
And there's an airplane rising. From such a height
The world must seem a shadowy minnow pool.
I am a small darkness stirring the shadows.
I move toward the silent house, awash in silence.

FIRST BOOK

I stood alone in my study holding the book,
Flipping the pages, their edges riffling beneath
My thumb which shook a little as poem by poem

Things unreconciled fluttered before me,
A stereopticon of words, their meanings
Forcing to mind an image of flashing lights—

A trailer truck overturned on an icy hill
At night, phosphorous flares spluttering hot
White light at intervals along the gleaming road,

A trooper's flashlight dancing erratic patterns
Like a red bee, as he keeps the traffic moving,
The revolving blue lights of the patrol car

Sweeping the scene, a still and sickly glow
Over the wreck, over the trooper's face
As, far off, the ambulance wails nearer

And the trooper bends toward him still pinned inside.

AFTER THE WINDSTORM

The popping snarl of chain saws punctuates
My grimly eulogistic thoughts of trees
Splintered and toppled. Dark furies, darker fates,
Have strewn our lawn with leafy similes,
These broken boughs, that shattered trunk, and now
White sawdust rising breathlike on the sun.
The foreman lifts his hard hat, wipes his brow.
This deed that's done will not really be done
Until specific consequences make
Specific claims, not only rank decay
But absence, absence. The saws stop. Coffee break.
Two orange trucks will haul it all away.
I think of another windless morning. You said,
"A time to die, another to be dead."

CODA

Tonight the windshield's dark,
Opaque with fog. I flick the switch
And the wipers clear our vision, a double arc
Like love and fear. Do you know which is which
Dear son, dear daughter, sleepyheads?
You've slept in strange new beds.

I drive slowly. Between
My house and yours our time is up,
Therefore I list the things we've done and seen—
Have we had fun? You answer together, "Yup!"
And I can grin. This weekend I've
Believed that we'll survive.

A judge decreed that you
Shall be with me on weekends, and
For supper every Wednesday, and for two
Full weeks each summer. Children, the witness stand
Was like a pew. *Thy will be done* . . . .
I sued for time, and won.

I cannot tell you why
This thing has been, but truly hell
Has seldom sustained such fury. We horrify
Nature and, yes, ourselves with anger. Well,
That's over. Enough. The fist somehow
Goes weak and opens. Now

Here is your house, I send
You in with your duffle bags and black
Fat teddy bears, and call, "Goodbye till Wednesday," then bend
As you drop everything and both come running back—
We cling to what we now dare miss.
For each a hug, a kiss,
A life of this.

MILL RIVER

Well, children, we're here again today
To hear the cadence of water over stone,
The pines sighing, the busybody jay,
To parse the insects' tireless monotone,
To eat our picnic lunch. It's August 1st,
We've had two hours to get love said somehow.
In March we saw that elm stump at its worst,
Slimy with rot. It's sprouting mushrooms now.

Throw twigs into the water, I'll watch them bob
Downstream as brave as words. Throw pebbles, too,
I'll watch them skip and sink. My harder job
Is shaping such a silence as must do
To answer, *Why?* I turn you toward the door
Beyond which all the world is metaphor.

THE TRIPLE STAR

Twenty-four trillion miles from it, I pore
Over its spectrograph. Alpha Centauri burns
Three separate lives. The cosmos of metaphor
Expands and lights new signs of old concerns.
The outer star completes one orbit of
The waltzing central pair in a million years,
The data of astrophysics conjures love
Which magnifies our needs and all their heirs—

My son, my daughter, point to the triple star:
Three stable orbits, light, and gravity's
Thrice-vacant heart the common center. Are
Not single loves expressed in wheeling threes?
Three orbits, one still center. Strange, but true.
It cannot change except as three stars do.

OF SCHOLARSHIP, DIVORCE, AND LUNCH

I've taken my daughter out to lunch today,
Met her at school and squired her straight to
The Lord Jeffrey Amherst Inn: a plate
of three cheeses, a slice of country pâté,
Eggs Benedict, salad. We talk about her new
Career as a student (Not good, she grins, but *great*),

I learn this kindergartner's first week in
That world she's longed for, for a long, long time.
The older kids had left her at home for years,
But now she's ridden the yellow bus, she's been
Called on, recessed, she's clutched her shiny dime
For milk, she's watched a little girl shed tears

For mommy, mommy, mommy. She tells of this
Wide-eyed, yet mature, and somehow I,
As fathers learn to do, keep a straight face.
Our coed waitress dotes, loath to miss
One word this scholar says, and says, *my, my,*
But *sotto voce*. The Inn stands next to Grace

Episcopal Church, in which my scholar goes
To Sunday School—not *school* to her, for there
She only sings some hymns and finger paints
And watches Mom dispense the coffee. But those
Stories about the Lord have made a fair
Impression on her mind, and the lives of saints,

And certain words, *martyr,* and *Nazareth.*
These trouble the little spirit into thought.
It is a miraculous thing to answer need
As Jesus did, with parables and death,
She thinks, or somehow feels, her brow a knot
Of moral lessons. This year, she'll start to read.

Our waitress hovers, bound to chat awhile,
To ask her age and read us the desserts.
Who will my daughter be at twenty-one?
I try to imagine her grown, to reconcile
This waitress with my five-year-old. It hurts
To think of all she'll learn. It's all begun.

I order sherbet, and look around the room
At Department lunches, lunch-loves, lunch interviews,
A haze of smoke above the talk and clink
Of silverware on china. At one, the heirloom
Corner clock goes *bong,* a piece of news
That turns at least two dozen heads. "I think

I'm getting sleepy," and sure enough she's slid
Down in her chair, the thumb starts up, but she brings
Manners to mind, and grins, sheepish. I see
We'll have to skip the sherbet, which never did
Arrive—there goes our waitress now—she flings
Her pad and pen on the desk and angrily

Stalks across the room, straight for the door,
Her face flushed, her eyes streaming, her hands
fists at her sides. *She's quit,* I think, *she's quit—*
The hostess pursues the waitress now, more
Flustered with every step, then stops and stands
Gaping out at the street. She's gone. The pit

Of my stomach tells me violence was done,
Was spoken in the restaurant's kitchen or,
Perhaps, by telephone. We get up to go.
The hostess has our check. I pay. Does one
Tip the waitress? The hostess says, "Oh, sure,
I'll hold it for her here. She's ill." "Oh,"

I say, and stoop to take my scholar's hand.
She didn't see what happened, her back to it all.
We leave, breathing the hostess's perfume.
Crossing the sunlit Common, I understand
Little of life. My daughter skips. It's Fall,
The first red leaves drop brightly to their doom.

THE FLORAL EGG

Her love, so faintly whispered, comes to this
Still world of metaphor between the poles
Of a blown and painted egg, its genesis
Suspended by one gold thread through two pinholes:
Exotic petals in lacquered pastel inks
Cling to a surface white as thoughts of death.
As love alone sustains frail worlds, she thinks
Those crucial truths that hold love like a breath:

That light may dwell within the things we say;
That words are surfaces thin as the mist
On eyes that by the common light of day
Rejoice in vision; that certain truths exist
In nearly weightless forms, because they must,
And may at any moment turn to dust.

DAY MOON

1.

I think of how, this morning, you stooped to lift
Your white silk nightgown up from the floor. You were
Naked, your face abstracted, the linen curtains
Luminous white behind you, your body outlined
Against the morning light like fire-lit copper,
Sweet as russet apples, the curve of your breast
Making my mind a zither. You straightened, turning,
Dropping the nightgown on the bed, then smiled
That inward smile you smile recalling pleasure.

2.

I think of how a certain gesture will tease
A tensile music out from hesitant light,
How sometimes you will stand there at the window
Watching the dawn, pale gray and pale blue shadows,
Your fingertips lightly tapping the window frame
Seeming to find time's metronomic time,
Seeming to draw the rapt natural world
Close to your body, the first white daylight flowing
In through the window, swirling at your feet
As seafoam swirled and sighed at the feet of Venus.

3.

I think of how, on summer afternoons,
You wash your hair at our old-fashioned sink,
Barefoot, in rolled-up jeans, your bare back bent,
Your hands buried in soap. The water is running,

You turn your head from side to side, rinsing
That three-foot rope of foaming golden light,
A pale Susanna bathing. And when you turn,
Bare-breasted, tying the towel around your hair,
I am no gawking Elder. No, I am
Earth's ordinary god, bemused by beauty.

4.
A pale day moon rises over the trees,
Love's silver thumbprint, that faint identification
Of who we are who listen, listen, trying
Phrase by phrase to score familiar voices,
Dream, touch, remembrance. A hushed afternoon,
That symbol rising faintly over the world,
These visions of you refracted from common daylight—
My mind has played the body's music gladly.
You nap in the next room, about to waken.
A pale day moon rises over the trees.

NEARER

I remember how you knocked, once, at my door,

Stood in the dim hallway, leaned against me
In stillness, a long stillness, and then you sighed,
Gently as a leaf falling, a flutter of breath,

My memory of that breath a faint imprint
On the white surface of time, a fossil there:
Leaf, fern, or the bones of a small fish.

Somewhere a spider web swayed because you sighed.

I remember how you sat in the rocking chair
And did not rock, your head tilted, listening
To cricket song, that weak voice that was,

Surely, there in the gathering October dusk,
The summer's last song, the diminished dirge
You wanted then, listening, your head tilted.

Somewhere, because you listened, a birch tree shivered.

The room was like an abandoned stone chapel.
You stood, moved to the window, and gazed out
Into the dusk, nearer the darkening world.

A LITTLE NIGHT MUSIC

I watch the still snow falling over the harbor,
The flat black water speckled with mooring lights
And wharf lights, winking reds, whites, and greens,

The harbor held in the arms of such a stillness
As you would recognize—yes, you—as dark
As that dark word you held beneath your tongue

Month after month, that word you could not speak
Nor swallow all that time. On the phonograph
The *Nachtmusik* is playing over and over,

I stand at the window, which is at night a mirror
As well as window, looking through my reflection,
Watching the still snow fall over the harbor.

Behind me, in this room you know so well,
The *Nachtmusik* you know so well, before me
The tide half out, the channel bells all silent:

I stand at the window watching for a long time,
My reflection blurred now by melting snow
That runs in droplets down the glass, glistening

By harbor lights and the dim lamplight behind me.
I feel your absence leaning against my body,
Its arms around me. I feel its gentle breathing.

The *Nachtmusik* concludes, begins again.
At last I think, *There's no such thing as silence* . . .
And feel the words fall toward you, like night snow

That melts touching the surface of the harbor.

AUBADE FLORESCENT

I lean against the bathroom sink,
   My head throbbing. Sick,
Hung over, I open the mirror door,
   Wince at its dull click,

And stare at the shelves on which I keep
   The things that keep flesh whole:
Aspirin, Band-Aids, yellow salve,
   But nothing for the soul,

Nothing at all but floss and powder,
   Scissors, eyedrops, gauze—
My head's throbbing, my eyes burning.
   I breathe deeply. This pause,

Always, before I gulp the pills
   That nudge my headache up
And back a foot or so, out
   Behind my head: the cup

Of water now, the aspirin swallowed,
   Chalky. I think of the gold
Smolder of bourbon, quintessential heat
   Of sunshine twelve years old—

Ah, bourbon, bourbon's an alchemy,
    Distillers alchemists,
The lead of loneliness made gold
    As blood thumps in my wrists,

Ah, bourbon, bourbon, burning bush,
    Teleology is
The faithful drinker's weeping for
    Some voice to answer his.

The lead of loneliness made gold
    Too briefly: bourbon ordains
Stuporous sleep, wherein gold words
    Turn leaden in the veins,

A desolate sleep wherein the heart's
    A cratered satellite
Circling, rocking the gray blood's tide
    With all its sagging might.

I shut the cabinet door. It clicks.
    Everything's in its place.
How cold the mirror's surface is,
    The image of my face.

POST-OP

To hear those wrens, even that crow! Now,
months after entering conditioned air, I breathe
the grass in, leaves, clover, the sweet, so sweet,
sour of dandelions, a whole world found
intact. The roughness of bark. Two sea gulls labor
east toward the ocean. Acorn. Chestnut. Pine cone.
The sun plays pizzicato on my eyelids.
Fragrance of mossy tree trunks. Nothing's still,
nothing's silent. I chew on a blade of grass
feeling myself a breathless thrilled quintet
of senses in the morning air—color
sings and sings for the joy of it, and touch
and smell join in, and the taste of grass. I hear
the rustling of cattails, and read this gate: an X,
and X marks the sanctifying spot.
I push it open, step into the wildflower meadow
where a faint scent of ocean tinctures the breeze.
Earth turns in sunlight. I walk the earth, intact.

IV. AT LARGE

TALE TO TELL
February 14, 2002

In brilliant morning sunshine,
at the bus stop, waiting:
a pint bottle, Seagram's, smashed
on the sidewalk, a fan
of scattered glassglint, the label
holding bits of it together as,
near to the glass, blown against
the foot of a wrought iron fence,
a petite pink bra shivers
in the variable breeze of this
crystal-cold Valentine's morning.

TRESPASS

The farmer is dead,
Four sons went south from here
And never came back. A white bone lies
Beside the steps, and a red
Enamelled teapot. The day moon's sheer
Gentle persistence pries
Gray roof boards loose, and the iron bed
Despised by them now gone
Rusts on a lawn

Grown three feet high.
I know this house, I learned it
By nightmare's baffling rote: the squeak
Of leaning beams, the cry
Of anguished hinges, the scent and grit
Of plaster dust in bleak
Dry dreamless rooms that flatly deny
The swamps of flesh and fear.
Now I am here.

Rank goldenrod
Has undermined the porch,
Grapevines loosen the shingles. first pride
Then passion failed. Spent pod,
Discarded trunk, extinguished torch—
This house once magnified
A young wife and the village god.
Now brash woodpeckers drill
The posts and sill.

I shoulder the doors
That open on broken walls
And curtains shredded on window frames.
A hollow wind implores
My shadow, as it slides and stalls,
To whisper the ruined names—
Their rooms, their tools, their meals and chores—
My shadow, bent on the stair:
Trespasser, heir.

AN ELM LEAF

This is New England's finest light, the chill
Brilliance of quartz, the white clapboard houses
Nearly translucent now. A brown leaf
Veined with darker brown clings and shivers
Here on its branch that reaches toward the pond,
A brittle tongue telling November's moods
And themes, the thin prophetic voice which is
Ours for the slow transcription of the code.

We've heard it all before, yet somehow we must
Attend the single leaf or forfeit November
To bronze and velvet, the coffin of abstract thought.
This was a swollen reddish-purple bud
Burst at last by green, the pale leaf
Unfurling toward the weightier green of August,
Limp with the ponderous sullen fullness of
Exhausted knowledge, then stunned by early frost,

Its gold and scarlet apocalypse, then rain,
Rain, cold, and this eventual brown.
I'm standing now beneath the leaf, hearing
Its stubborn voice, squinting against the light
Beyond the branch, the sunlight wrinkling on
Water shining like uncrumpled tinfoil.
Winter is nearly on us. The leaf quivers
And clings, and I imagine a future for it:

The leaf skitters on white ice, then lies
Still on the sunstruck surface, absorbing warmth
The ice reflects, and as it does it warms
The ice beneath it, begins to sink, hour
By slow hour precisely impressing itself
A quarter-inch into the three-foot ice. It is
A fossil now, and I stare at it, thinking,
What else but this is poetry or prayer?

Each falling leaf numbers a human skull,
Billions of lives buried among the roots
Of one great tree, and the voices buried there
Have risen, will rise again and again to cry
With brittle tongues the prophecy of green.
A fugitive leaf skittering over ice
Or thin snowcrust: listen, now it is
A pen-nib scratching, a voice trapped in the air.

A BOX TURTLE

1.

His swamp reeking behind him, dry woods ahead,
A turtle blunders toward the asphalt road.
The turtle in me shudders—there's little enough
Traffic here, and what there is goes slowly,
But his is an awful gamble all the same.

His claws scratch on the asphalt. He lifts his head
High as he can and, getting up on tiptoe,
Makes his lurching way. He looks silly,
The humped back, the bullet head. I imagine
Him on a train, holding a rolled umbrella.

And I've seen him in the natural history museum,
A species which has blinked dully at change
For millions of years. I've felt him tug at my fish line.
I've seen him squashed on a road near where I
Was a child. The child in me shudders and runs.

2.

The domed carapace shines in the sun, flecked
With orange and yellow, the red eyes shine like drops
Of his own blood. The hinged plastron beneath
Can lock his soft life tight, a pocket watch case,
A confidence the world will break but once.

3.

He's nearly halfway now, he falters, stops,
Inspects the yellow line, then crosses it.
He is a moving target crossing the still
Surface of his own death. He blunders into
The roadside grass, he blunders into the woods.

4.

And that's that. Or does his small success
Deserve a gesture, some acknowledgment
Beyond my inward sigh for vulnerable things?
Chances are he'll outlive me. By now
He's found a rotten log teeming with grubs.

He crawled from swamp to woods, his reasons his own,
While I walk home on the road he crossed, the swamp
Sour on my left, the sweet woods on my right,
And I hear behind me now the clank and clatter
Of Mr. Winter's mail truck, and here's my mailbox,

Its red flag up, poems inside, outgoing.

THE CARDINAL SINS: A BESTIARY

Wrath

Two bull moose locked their antlers. Locked unto death
They push, twist, pull, plow up the ground.
Soon they will fall, soon skeletons will gleam,
Blanched in the autumn sun, but now their breath
Steams on the air, and sunset burns profound
As judgment in their failing eyes. They seem
Unaware of crows perched waiting, one by one.
They struggle toward a beaked oblivion.

Sloth

Consider the clam half-sunk in yellow mud,
The bivalve mollusk. Surviving by design,
He reproduces life in which no move
Ever is willed, passivity the bud
And bloom of flesh. The locked thing is a shrine
To indolence, its morphology a reproof
To me, who picks it up: an impervious, crude
Shell guaranteeing jellied lassitude.

Pride

We watch the pet iguana's murky eye.
He watches us, watches us through what is
Millions of years of arrogance. We dare
Not touch his dinosaur back—its ridges defy
The hackled brain once to forget that his
Ancestors tore up trees. We will beware.
He turns, faces the sun, his colorless
Cold eye a fact. The world will acquiesce.

Avarice

A cancer virus entered the lung and slipped
Into the bloodstream. It kissed a red cell,
Subverted its nucleus, altered, one by one,
The DNA molecules. It deftly stripped
An atom here, another there, life fell
To parasitic life. Its code undone,
The cell divides. The virus thrives, enshrined
Within its wealth of replicating kind.

Lust

The caged monkey yowls at his sister, who,
A cage away, refuses him glance or thought.
He starts once more to masturbate and shriek,
And, as his semen spurts, splattering to
The path between their cages, she stares at the spot.
Shall he turn into a swan? He turns a bleak
Expression toward his limp and dripping gland,
And mutters to himself, and licks his hand.

Gluttony

The grub worm eats his tunnel, inches by yards
Through humus soil, digesting as he goes
The nutrients of Earth, leaving behind
A slippery line of excrement. He guards
His cosmic view with blindness—the grub worm knows
Increase of self requires an austere mind,
Belief is singular. He measures time
By slow conversion. His history is slime.

Envy

The fakir squats beside his begging bowl.
I watch the cobra rise, drawn by the flute
Above the basket's rim, the music swaying
Its hooded head, its tongue flicking. Man's whole
Mind loathes a lidless eye, that cold, acute,
Pale amber vision. The mendicant is playing
Death for coins. Slowly I recognize
My body as it sways in the cobra's eyes.

A HUMMINGBIRD

Electric in green-tipped feathers the hummingbird
Whirs from the lilac bush, and I pursue
My blistering terror of its sound: no word
For flight or danger does what thin wings do—
The rasping of opacity on white air,
The dry current, a buzz and whine that clings
Close to the scalp—heat lightning under the hair
Spits till the *dura mater* sizzles and stings.

What charges so small a thing with so much fear?
Is it too like an insect, too bright a design
Of needs and nerves and instincts far from mine,
Or something more? Again it whirs too near—
I shrink back from it, back in the green-edged pain
Of rotting jungles, shrill, deep in the brain.

OF NATURE

The cosmos is a millpond. Pitch
　　　　A pebble in, disturb
That mirror-surface over which
　　　　You lean: now noun and verb

Shiver to life—lean nearer, find
　　　　Images there, such things
As bring elusive moods to mind:
　　　　In spreading concentric rings

The silver crescent moon, the fleck
　　　　Of sunstruck bits of quartz,
The elm leaf shadows brushing your neck,
　　　　A chipmunk's shrill retorts

To distant thunder. Now contemplate
　　　　Pale Vega and the still
Spectral sprawling of novae—wait,
　　　　Listen: a whippoorwill,

Her soft and thousand-parted note
　　　　Of ease and eagerness
Familiar to your lips and throat,
　　　　For you have whispered *Yes*.

Behold the sensible world and touch
　　　　Whatever is with thought,
Creating, then, Creation, much
　　　　As Adam's voice begot

A world by naming things, as Eve
    Created fate when she
Gazed at the subtle twist and weave
    Of vines, and what would be,

As you have done. The water is clear
    And there you are, who turn
Toward life now, in your hand a mere
    And mythic sprig of fern,

And as you turn the breathing world
    Tenses—beyond the wall
A pheasant rises, the bright air swirled
    By thrashing brilliance all

Symbolic in the sun, the thrill
    Of definition in his
Purple and red ascent, until
    Meaning is all there is.

OF ART

The moon's phases arc in red
      Across the cave's black wall,
A bleeding bull lowers his head
      Above your head. You crawl

On hands and knees to know these things,
      You crouch in the cave. Now
Imagine the hunter as he sings
      And smears blood on his brow,

And hear, too, worlds and worlds away,
      The Pharaoh's finger tap
His son's death mask. His breaths outweigh
      That gold face on his lap.

And hear a brush whisper across
      Rice paper, pale blue inks
Shadowing greens and browns, the moss
      Surrounding a man who thinks

Such thoughts as are the picture's stream
      And bending trees, his cloak
A fading blue, his mist-green theme
      The world, told stroke by stroke.

Your flashlight beam bisects the cave,
      The limestone blackened so
By greasy smoke. That same fire gave
      Us Michelangelo—

His hopes fragile, hourglass clocks,
    His bones the hissing sand,
He stands among the marble blocks
    With calipers in his hand,

And even now his eyes prepare
    The limbs which must survive
Stone agony, a body where .
    The thought of life will thrive.

We ask of art the world.
    We create ourselves in it.
Imagination will ever be
    By darkness wildly lit,

Dark and the hunter's song and shout.
    Art is barely begun.
Turn off your flashlight now, crawl out
    And praise the hunter's sun.

HENRI MATISSE: "THE GREEN LINE"

I imagine him sitting at his easel, Henri
The troubled fauvist. How far will the painter go
Beyond the world he lives in? To that degree
That green subdues his overwhelming sorrow.
I hear him breathing. The canvas of his wife
Is finished now and, staring at what he's done,
He slowly wipes the paint from his palette knife.
He thinks, This could be true of anyone.

At first the green line stunned him, but now it has
Convinced the rhythms deepest in his mind.
He rubs a bare foot on the gritty floor
Then tilts his chair back, balancing, rocking as
He thinks that art is sometimes very kind.
For now he dares not add his signature.

HEAD OF A WOMAN

1.

Her face is strange. We sense that she is wise,
A woman troubled but wise, troubled but kind.
The shadowy introspection of her eyes
Complicates her half-smile: she may be blind,
Or may recall something that makes her sad.
I hold the head, two pounds of reddish clay,
And stare at it, wondering if she had
Some long anguish. She chooses not to say.
Outside, a breeze moves through the elm. It stirs
The leaves to music, a pale fantasia, hers.

2.

Her head is tilted, listening, first to the leaves,
Then for some audible memory of names
We too may recognize. Listening retrieves
Those certain sounds, they make their certain claims,
The smile plays at her mouth. And on her lean
Angular face we see the need to cry:
It seems that she has lived her life between
A wish for song, a wish for silence. We try
To recognize the loss kept private there,
But fail. It is, for now, her own affair.

3.

The breeze moves in the elm, and here on the floor
The elm leaf shadows play a version of
The woman's thought. The patterns there are more
Inclined to repetition than such a love
As hers would have them, but only slightly so:
Intricate repetition, dark on light
And light on dark, and we begin to know
How trouble in her mind affected sight.
This altering of sun and shade requires
Relinquishment of something she desires.

4.

What is it we have felt? Affinity,
Perhaps, with this sadness we find we know.
Our breathing fills her shadowed reverie.
Yes, she who sculpted this head wanted to show
A hesitancy of mind: as her thin hand
Moved on the face, the face slowly took on
The hesitancy of hands. We understand
A sadness approaching, a gladness not quite gone,
The smile lingering. Her steady inward gaze
Translates the leaves' fantasia, phrase by phrase.

ERIK SATIE: *TROIS GYMNOPEDIES*

1.

Each remnant, isolated note expresses
Specific pain, the exacting words, perhaps,
Two spoke while walking a city street
Through darkness, from pool to pool of lamplight, hand
In weakening hand, that failing touch recalled
In these bass chords which punctuate the brief
Hesitant thoughts, the footsteps hesitant.

2.

The sadness of the melody, remote
As suburban hills twinkling across a river,
Conjures a purple evening air in which
The near and delicate will thrive, the sadness
Not of sad church-bells, nor sad foghorns,
Nor traffic sounds, nor the rise and fall of voices,
But fingertips tapping lightly on a wineglass.

3.

The theme begins to verge toward resignation.
The notes become like strangers on a platform,
Each aware of the others, each certain now
That nothing at all can save it from its silence.
The music disengages from the world,
Drawing around itself an intimate darkness.
The notes become an auditory Braille.

TAO CHI: "OLD GINKGO AT MOUNT CH'ING-LUNG"

The shattered trunk looks dead, but life revives,
A new branch at the top, another near
The arthritic roots of this wreck of a tree:
New life from old, an image of the lives
Of i-min painters. Smashed by storms in the year
400, it lives in 1703.

Manchu invaders outlawed the ancient way,
But Tao Chi painted this, the surprising leaves,
Concealing in his strokes traditions banned
By arrogant marauders. His two boughs say
A man may chuckle even as he grieves,
New life from old, survival, this triumph and

A flock of swallows rising, as if to fly
All over China carrying the news
Of Tao Chi's ginkgo. The hills are brown and bare,
They rise into the blankest slate-gray sky:
There is no way an *i-min* could confuse
The meaning of the boughs and swallows there.

The swallows seem to rise out of the ground,
Out of the old tree's roots. Indeed, they do.
I wonder what Tao Chi was thinking then,
How his face might have crinkled, how the sound
Of his chuckling must have startled old Ming-lu
As she prepared the fish for Manchu men,

And must have startled the Manchu as they sat
In Tao Chi's garden, suspicious now, afraid
That they are being laughed at. But all they see
Is Tao Chi sitting gravely on his mat
Before the curious picture he has made,
The lightning-blasted trunk of a ginkgo tree.

I imagine the painter's chuckle spreading, I hear
A covert epidemic. Manchu knives
Are useless, baffled warlords sense delight
All over China. Such faith, Tao Chi, the mere
Image of what it is, will save our lives:
Two living boughs, and swallows taking flight.

A GIFT

1.

This orchid of blown glass, this artifact
Translucent as remembrance, yields the strange
Optics of sorrow. You turn it and refract
A brilliancy from loss, you rearrange
The qualities of mourning. And as you tease
Pale spectra out of sunlight, your thoughts are of
A way to alter thought, and by degrees
This alteration wakes the mind to love.

2.

You raise it toward the window, cheek and lips
Brushed by the quarter-tones of afternoon,
You turn the stem in those same fingertips
That plucked at tears and traced the crescent moon
On misted glass, then draw it toward your ear
As if the petals whispered, and as you do
The orchid becomes a seashell. Listen, hear
The harboring of themes derived from blue.

3.

Your eyes are closed, but darkness must defer
To urgent beauty, and by this deference
Old sympathies revive. You thought you were
Afraid, but beauty plays a syntax tense
As counterpoint whose meaning you construe
From flickering eyelids—not evidence of dream
But of desire, so long now overdue
That hushed acceptance abrogates a scream.

4.

The artist holds our clear devotions in
His fragile hands, and into those hands we
Commit our lives. Now, far beyond the din
Of what we know, the convulsed cacophony
Of populations playing rage, despair,
Noble illusion, greed, and all the rest,
Imagined beauty takes you unaware.
You look, and what you are is manifest.

THE EXPULSION
After a Painting by Judith Glantzman

1.

On this large canvas two red figures suffer the first
Intensity of being, the pain they feel like sea-spray
In that primordial air through which they try to move,
The stunned female reaching out toward him who stomps
Away from her, from us, into a disastrous weather.
There is no sense of time here, for them nor us, unless

This instant is time's quintessential germ, its seed,
An instant with no past, no future yet, only prime
Red conflict now: their agony like sea-spray breaking
Against the continents of such desire as must,
Surely for us as well as them, conclude in rage.
They find no syllable to tempt them back to language,

Nor have they any world but this one. Each rages, *I*.

2.

No! writhes in their clenched fists, and again, *No!*
We sense that writhing word, we clench it: the *I* that is
The picture's shrill affirmative, its crackling hope,
Its maniacal hymn, has risen to such a pitch as must
Condemn the world to misery, and these red figures
Prefigure us who shrink from them, the human mother

A woman reaching out, about to plead or weep,
Her left foot wrapped in hide, dried-blood brown, a

Crude boot she will always drag on her clumsy way
If she pursues the male (that choice an instant hence)
Who turns away hunched in his own vermilion trouble,
A thick-bodied Neanderthal-like Adam. There's no serpent

Unless the picture's awful silence is a serpent.

3.
We study the background, a complex texturing of white
With areas of blue-gray, intimating that time is
Tin- or slate-colored where the male is madly headed,
An eerie atmosphere, the subject of her gesture
Warning him back, forgiving, begging, but he is deaf
In outrage, stalking off as if to a crime of passion

Which she has instigated in his boiling marrow.
The little wisps of green he's leaving, unimportant,
Counted as nothing but a trifle of the world,
Are actually so crucial they will haunt the species
For twenty million years. Green indicates the plain
On which the female stands a long moment longer.

She reads his blotched red back in horror: fury bared.

4.
Quick as a chisel, this picture divides the gray mind
Of one standing before it, like splitting open a geode,
Exposing a glittering cosmos: the finite mind is opened

And thought brushes against the prismatic crystal myth
Of an uncorrupted infinite, a concealed eternal.
But two red human figures, crowned with their own loss,

With silence, with isolation (these words leaping to mind
So easily, so aptly) force us to flesh and blood:
Will wrestlers relax at last into embrace? Can brute
Bone clubs, prototype of the scepters raised by all
Death's messengers to the world, become the white batons
Raised to the hymns the geode heart holds hushed? These

Red figures crown creation with their wordless rage.

5.
What fruit did male and female eat? Knowledge of time
Frames them in startling agony, this silence cruel
As banishment, each moment made a flaming sword—
Each heartbeat's a weapon here, the angel's fiery threat
Keeping them from the cool green Paradise that they
Remember now with bitter little sneer-like thoughts

That now elect self-loathing's bleeding mouth, the mouth
To sing their separate hymns in praise of *I* and *I*.
She hesitates in the foreground, her arm raised. He
Abandons it all, barges into an atmosphere
Tense as a prayer, but strident with discordances
That lacerate his brain, dislocate his memories.

He stomps into history. She'll follow. We've begun.

V. TENTATIVE

DESERT WATCH

For twenty thousand years I've hunched beside
Smoldering coals, each new horizon gray
Then pink and gold. At last I've learned to read
the pulse of embers, and now I must decide
Whether or not to tell her, what to say.
My wife sleeps off the footsore life we lead,
Swollen with child. I know it now, it's true:
This desert is endless. I've done what I had to do.

ABRAHAM AT THE RUINS OF HAI

*And he went on his journeys from the south even
to Bethel, unto the place where his tent had
been at the beginning, between Bethel and Hai.*

GENESIS 13:3

1.

All the watchman's challenges gone. The priest's chant
Silenced. Dawn held hushed: like the depths of held breath
After sounds of struggle, a groan of hinges,
      Click of a bronze latch.

Time's enormous vacantness, tense with one sound:
Lean as fright, the buzz of an early locust
Burns the dawn's cool flesh in a temple ringed with
      Turrets of darkness.

But the locust finishes. I alone am
Held in Time's deep breathing. Shreds of night now
Ride the mist's wide rising, and with the sun a
      Closing of great doors.

2.

Veils of sunlight drift on the air above stiff
Wreckage: Hai burned to the ground, the charred beams
Heaped like ruined hopes in the hearts of old men.
      This was a city,

This was what men made of their dread of silence.
Thousands raised this cry that collapsed in wild fire—
Piles of voices, carcass of safety, splintered
     Bones of a false god.

Now the seasons turn in their endless patience,
Soothe the closing wound in the landscape's belly.
Now the hill winds linger beneath the trees, all
     Outrage forgotten.

Men will fear their days, will refuse their lifetimes.
Every beam and brick was of terror. Men raise
Not the spirit's voice, nor its symbol; men raise
     Walls of denial.

Yet, a man will come to his life at last. They
Stood one morning staring at this, their wrecked walls:
Dying, each alone with his death, the men heard
     Terrible heartbeats.

3.
I perceived my spirit in chance encounters:
Baffling footprints frozen in mud: a bare tree
Clutching spring's thin moon in its brittle arms; my
     Warning turned echo.

I declared my spirit: a drop of cool dew
Bending silver light from the morning's body
Casts an infinitesimal proof in hues deemed
      Hopelessly precious.

I divined my spirit: a rock of silence
Held beloved by terrible roots; in darkness,
Deep within this anguish of flesh, the roots seek
      Steadily downward.

Nothing thus known lasts. Save in one encounter
Only searching stays in my eyes. Then ask this:
Man, have you proved life? Have you seen your own eyes
      Mirrored in Death's eye?

4.
Here the Jordan River is crawling southward,
Past the crumbling walls. It discerns its dim way,
Valleys, plains, an intricate way. The white sun
      Dazzles its surface.

Slow with purpose: steadily seeking southward,
South to thick salt depths, the insistent ripples
Tremble, turn uncertain beneath a low bough's
      Moment of shadow.

This: the current, holding a course through wide years,
Weighs diminished pebbles in hands of hushed praise,
Probes desire's deep burden of change: a slow thought
       Moving in God's mind.

5.
Terah's death began on a windy spring day.
I was five years old, I was holding his staff,
Then—as we sat there on the mossy rock, a
       Father and his son

Tending thirty goats on a grassy hillside—
Then I saw my father, I knew what he was:
Dying moved like weather across his lined face,
       Decades of weathers

Drifting past his eyes while his gaze ranged far off.
Then he put his hand on my shoulder. I said,
"Father shall you die?" and he answered, "I am
       Young in my son's blood."

Terah's days were full with the sun and hill winds.
Yet, his spirit lay as a field of boulders,
Wide and strewn with griefs that would not be broken.
       Nobody walked there.

Terah's death was quiet. His people mourned him.
Father, I have walked in your spirit, I have
Wandered seven years in the fields of boulders
        All over Canaan—

Father, I have measured my life through your eyes.
Shall I feel your breath in my spirit? Shall I
Learn your steady voice? And are these your answers:
        Shuddering silence

Up from Sheol's gloom, and the Negeb death-wind
Blowing all night long from the south, and rolling
Darkness shaped by hills, and the reeling night sky—
        Nothing but silence?

Father, I stood still in the fields at dusk.
Always I have whispered your name—I waited,
Listened: silence throbbed in the rock; a light wind
        Rattled the thistles.

Father, in me all of your hopes have come to
Thoughts like withered roots, and my flesh is crumbling.
Now my stiff voice shakes in the wind, and silence
        Throbs in my parched heart.

6.
Build. The silence begs me to build. But build what?—
All I build is silence itself: it finds me,
Haunts me. Stone by stone I have built; the altars
        Mock me in chorus.

What belief is taken in nets of labor?
Who has caught one hour in the mesh of his days?
Which of your hymns stayed in the web of silence
        Spanning your spirit?

Yet, the silence begs me to build, requires it.
Your response to silence shall be your life: build.
Knowing silence, how shall a man speak? How build,
        Knowing destruction?

7.
Life is held like fruit in the boughs of dying—
Who desires that tree? Who desires? He speaks it.
Slowly his new utterance sinks, a small stone
        Trying the silence.

Fires upon the mountain, the plain, the desert,
Man among the shadows of trees, of rocks; his
Haunted lips have cracked, and they bleed to slow prayer
        Trying the silence.

Weeping waits like fog in the mountain shadows.
Joy would curl like smoke toward the breathless midnight.
Trying dark by dark in his vague directions,
    Trying the silence,

Man, the same lost man in a thousand places,
Strange, and stranger still to himself, the slow lips
Lost in pain and murmuring, lost without prayer
    Trying the silence,

Man describes the fog in the mountain shadows,
Man, who tells the smoke on the breathless midnight:
Slowly each new utterance sinks, a small stone
    Trying the silence.

8.
Here the Jordan River is crawling southward,
South to thick salt depths. I have waited nine days,
Listening. One word uttered could charge my waiting
    Vivid with purpose.

Will the shadows, rising together, sing truth?
Will the dust teach justice, or promise justice?
Will the broken bones of a city whisper
    Wisdom to strangers?

Only slow, mute shadows, approach of evening,
Now the ninth day ends. I will go. The late sun
Probes the cooling violet, weeds and rubble.
　　　Here, where the gates stood,

Threads of light's pale shining attach to two beams,
Span the angle made in their fall. A brief air
Tests the pattern, tentative: all the web gleams,
　　　Shivers a sheer grief.

CODA

3:00 A.M.

My candle gutters, dims. What's there to see?
The moth tapping the windowpane may be
The knuckle of the One, beckoning me.

FROM THE LOW DUNGEON

I called upon thee: thou saidst,
Fear not.
LAMENTATIONS 3:57

Love's simple answer gleamed, a blade.
Quick, at my wrists, the rope was cut.
The rope was silence. Bound, I prayed:
Love's simple answer gleamed, a blade
Released me. Am I now less afraid?
Cell walls remain, locks, sentries—but
Love's simple answer gleamed, a blade
Quick at my wrists. The rope *was* cut.

AUBADE

As hushed as nuns pressing God to their lips,
As deliberately as when great musics start,
The dawn extends itself, a rose light slips
Through mists that hold familiar forms apart:
Two courtyard lemon trees stand mute, as still
As thoughts of what they are, but they remain
Vague, vague as all things were before the mill
Of language ground the world from Adam's brain.

My breath mists on the window, I look out
On imminence as—nearer, nearer—it
Gives way to names, scant words which make me doubt
The simplest intimacy: kitchens are lit,
A shrimper thumps and chugs across the bay...
Morning begins with all the world to say.

AVE, VALE

The coffin enters Customs, and we assume
The hard transport of love in words that strain
Like cargo nets slung from the derrick-boom,
Raising the tonnage dockward. Can we explain
This passage? Two silent circling gulls divide
Life from the thought of life above steel ships;
And, soon or not soon, love will choose which side,
Will move or fail to move our moistened lips.

A diesel motor idles, a chain falls slack,
For one deep moment Commerce seems to pause.
We look far forward, cautious, we think back
Trying to know what vanished, what it was.

The coffin passes Customs, weighed, believed.

We sign for it, here, where it says *Received*.

ASHES

My father's ashes were scattered over the sands,
The windswept dunes he loved. For thirty years
I've thought of that and stared hard at my hands.
His breathing is oceanic in my ears.
Death asks us nothing, nothing at all, and yet
We ache to answer death with something true,
A voice will force its little rivulet
Of syllables over silence. My father knew

The mountain we must move is not our doubt
 But awesome certainty risen in the brain.
Ashes blow over sand, are blown without
A name or children, a voice, a thing to gain.
We'd move mountains of silence. We ask a lot.
A trickling voice is all the means we've got.

THE CRY

But how could my throat contain that tangled sound
When we pushed through brush to a lowland field and saw
That iron shape?—an old, high-wheeled hay rake
Left there to rust, half-sunk in the muddy ground.
Years and its own dead weight were all its law
As it sank there, slow as knowledge of a great mistake.

COVER

A weasel's track,
Tracks of the running prey—
Beside the brook a bedlam of signs,
Quick struggle where the owl's attack
Fell from the half-born day
Leaving on mud the frenzied designs
Of claw and beating wing,
The electric sting

Of talons on
His back or neck that tore
Two tufts of fur out of his skin,
Yet he survived the critical dawn.
Scrambling, making for
Cover against oblivion,
Into the brush and gone,
The tracks go on.

Author's Acknowledgments

Heartfelt thanks to my editor, Helen Lang, whose thoughtful insights and influences have made this a better book; and to John D'earth for his meticulous work in preparation of the manuscript.

About the Author

The poems of Paul Smyth have appeared in magazines and journals including *The Atlantic Monthly* and *Poetry* (which awarded him the Dillon Memorial Prize). His first collection, *Conversions*, published in 1974 by the University of Georgia Press, was followed by two books of poems published by Abbatoir Editions and Pennyroyal Press, both illustrated by artist Barry Moser, and a collection of epigrams. Paul Smyth died in late 2006, just after completing last corrections on the manuscript for *A Plausible Light*.

Paul Smyth's *A Plausible Light* was designed by Barry Moser in the spring of 2007. Moser also drew and engraved the frontispiece portrait of the poet. The typefaces are Zapf Renaissance Antiqua and Nofret. Zapf Renaissance Antiqua was designed by Herman Zapf, one of the greatest lettering artists of modern times. It was designed for the German Scangraphic Dr. Böger GmbH in Hamburg, from 1984–1986. Nofret was designed by Gudrun Zapf von Hesse in 1984 and issued by Berthold Typefoundry in Berlin. Like her husband, she is a prodigious lettering artist and type designer. ❧ The paper is Mohawk Superfine. ❧ The book was printed by Sheridan Books in the summer of 2007.

.